The Desperate Eye

Kieana Curtiss

BookLeaf Publishing

Presentation by *BookLeaf Publishing*

Web: www.bookleafpub.com

E-mail: info@bookleafpub.com

ISBN: 9789357210539

First edition 2022

The Abyss

I've been backed into hell's corner
Facing the shadows on the wall.
Horrified of my manifestations,
Petrified of inferno's revelations.
I had casted 17 shadows.
In the abyss they are called demons.
suffocated by their energy
how formidable their synergy.
waltzing around to the beat of my wounding
Whispering vile things, painfully extruding
So weak I couldn't speak, but Providence gave
me power
"My soul you dare not Devour!
For what is it that you seek?!"
With great loathing the demons began to speak,
"Your infirmity is the cause of your damnation!"
"Hell bound you will be for eternity!!" The
demons bellowed with glee.
With great indignation I cried, "by whose
decree?!"
The fiends began to mutter incomprehensibly.
I stood hell casted with great trepidation.
My fate had been declared.
Ordained to discover the chasm of my soul,
purgatory made my sinkhole.

The Vessel

The demons carried me down to the ocean of chaos
Waves of flames grew with heightened intensity
Osiris, the ancient entity
Appeared as if reckoned by some unholy seance
With wings of fire, Osiris motioned towards me
I kneeled before the king of death and wept
“Osiris, how mighty is your spiritual throne that you rule both the underworld, and the spring of new life. Surely you can help me navigate my soul out of this dark and desolate night!”
The power of his voice was like thunder
The waves became still, and my soul stood asunder
“Aibqaa Makanak!” decreed Osiris.
There appeared before me a large vessel
"Step inside” he commanded.
"It has come time for you to enter upon your divine descent.
You will suffer immense crushing.
All designed for you to repent”.

The Hell fiends surrounded the vessel as Osiris casted his spell.

I was cursed into a paralysis, denied the power to repel
A raging river of fire carried my vessel into the 7th dimension of hell.

Desolation

Insurmountable desolation had overwhelmed me

Causing my wounds to erupt with great intensity

Vivid images emerged out of the darkness

My time on earth flashed before me with acute sharpness

There appeared before me the cause and effect of my wounding:

A child suffering from emotional neglect

Naked, alone, often she wept

Un-silenced cries

Neither tear dried

Loveless mother and father

Both lowly and defiled

The adolescent pacified

In search of men to beguile

Love and pain became one in the same

Remembrances of heartless declarations

Anything real was met with speculation

Ruthless quarrels, my wounding to blame

Longing to fill the void of love

Desperately in search for the lack thereof

In vain I cried "True Love is a lie! My heart
shall I guard until the day I die!"

Exasperation

My spirit wept

until the demon of anger was felt.

My eyes bled crimson red

Energetically charged like a wild beast

My deep rooted pain became anger's feast

In my paralysis, I could not flee

Cursed and damned for my iniquities

Å Worthless Brute

The blood and disfigured flesh of those I
obliterated filled the vessel

screams magnified with great intensity

Obscene brutality was my propensity

Maddened by their pain and anguish,

I laid powerless to vanquish

To Have been born in the flesh

My life did oppress

A worthless brute I had been with vicious
insanity

I began to curse myself with atrocious profanity

Yet, I realized there is no greater pain than to
deny thyself love

No greater tragedy than to endlessly search thereof

I had never felt more alone

This deep dark void is all I had ever known

Downcast for Refinement

I am bound to the abyss,

Downcast for refinement,

suffering for my misalignment

It is God I provoked

to rescind all hope

Made a soul without wings to fly

Captivated by demons ordained to chastise

Dejection

For where does one gain understanding?

To discern that which brings peace?

To discover what is cleansing to the soul, to make what is broken whole?

Underneath hell's feet, too great a burden for the answers I seek

Yet, still I possessed a perverted sense of hope.

I began to pray:

"Oh Holy Spirit. I lay here in complete stillness. I have suffered immensely for my misdoings. I understand, your holy majesty, I have been villainous. Please for—"

The demon of despair

motioned with an intensifying glare.

While still in my paralysis, the demon commanded, "Rise up hellhound!"

I remarked, “Leave me be, you orator of conspiracies!”

“I dare not!” The demon replied.

“You dwelled amongst the most wicked in the realm of the earth.

Your life’s work has been evil’s claim.

United by the blood of Lucifer, God you did defame.

How imprudent of you to now cry for salvation?!”

With great acrimony the demon grew belligerent.

“You preposterous hell spirit! Why have you begun to pray? It is all too late!

God is the one who inspired your deceit ,

your life pre-ordained to be a murderous cheat!

Anarchy your master, on earth and thereafter!

Inherently malevolent, dare I posit.

Surely, it is love that is the false prophet!"

"Faith is the spring of life!" I cried out. The magnetic pull towards goodness!

In my cocoon I was confined,

but to emphasize my freedom of mind!"

If given one more chance, love I shall find!"

I dare not fall under your spell!

To suffer for hell's cause , dare I stand and rebel!"

The fiend loathed, "Too late you ingrate!

You dwell amongst the wicked!

Ever fouled and sickened.

By your own creation is this Purgatory,

shall Lucifer reign in glory!"

Formed By Fear

The vessel turned to ash

And I was carried away by the raging river of fire

As if to purify a tarnished metal,

I was reduced to a fluid state

Unformed, and without expression.

The demon of fear accompanied my transgression

This demon was familiar to me during my time on earth

He had formed me into a monstrous creature

Though powerfully iniquitous

I was made fragile, and insubstantial

Encompassing a fear of exposure

For that meant my extinction,

Better for me to kill and to make no distinction

For what greater fear than to be regarded as a weakling?

Or an essence without grit?

Blood on my hands synonymous to my strength

Symbolizing my fear, I was so monstrously cavalier

The Green-Eyed Monster

So Grotesque was I formed, and
characteristically repulsive.

A distorted sense of self, reflected in green .

Assailing abominations , inciting malicious
incantations

It had been my character to delight in molesting

Indecent advances, romantically transgressing

Triggered by a deep insecurity, an attempt to
hide my obscurity

With no sense of value, better to demolish the
proud

Ever threatened by the highly esteemed

I eagerly disavowed

Transforming myself into a figure of desire,

I set out to be the succubus

eminence I'll acquire

how great did bitterness abide

that I enticed man to backslide?

It was my mission to tear apart

The lovers dream to unite in heart

Libidinous

Asmedous, the most powerful demon in the earthly realm,

how might his force in my life did he helm

Under his command, I gambled my sanctity,

I became a creature of conspicuous yearning .

Lascivious acts to entice, my wicked pleasure

A siren's ploy to enchant and charm

Gently, did my breasts, and caress disarm

My tongue like the tail of a serpent

I imparted flames that aroused

Asmedous made me his Lilith

Perversion to my divinity

While here in inferno's kingdom, he came within my vicinity

We united in carnal desire,

the demon of lust left me ablaze with fire

How intense its heat, flames burned dire

With lust as my master, I had proudly proclaimed

To promote the destruction of love

To leave isolated and empty

To render Lost souls aplenty

For it is lust that consumes the undisciplined life,

I laid ablaze in truth of this unlawful vice

Hubris

So many hearts I had devoured

I was supreme in my power

Full of pretension,

the fated cause of my descension

Cursed with manipulative charm

no wisdom could alarm

An insatiable appetite

in endless search for my delight

So cocksure

for what need was there to be pure?

Instant gratification did fill every void

Mingled with pride and cruelty

how my hubris alloyed

While still ablaze in flames

the demon of pride called my name

“She-demon! Dare I impose?

My ghostly form rose.

Oppressing my pride

the demon turned the tide

Allowing me to see the brute underneath

Destructive conceit

my affections deplete

Ever the narcissist

the time had come for my catharsis

Negation

At the root of my conceit

was the threat of inadequacy

Revealed to me by the demon of scarcity

I beheld the veracity

My incompetence and shame

heaven's angels to blame !

Gasping for validation

the intoxicating desperation

All fueled my psychopathy

Deepening depression

heightening apathy

Neither hope or faith could I ever regard

For fate had dealt me a heavy card,

from birth

the angels determined me best to discard

How unjust for me to now be damned?

To spend eternity in reprimand!

What control did I possess over my life's condition?

For where was Providence during my moments of contrition?

God the source of my being

did impart these deficiencies

Ah! The Demon of Falsehood was right!!

God formed me out of spite!

He who is supreme in power

the Source of all creation

Had made my earthly life one of negation

Lamentation

Ever more I lamented, “banned from paradise,
Oh how can that be?!

The demon of vengeance drew near to incite me.

“Oh Heaven dare I speak?!”

Appearing before me was Archangel Raziel.

“I am the gatekeeper of divine mysteries,
bearing supreme knowledge of every soul. For
what in your damnation do you dare to speak?”

Boldly I confessed, “To desecrate the accusers of
my soul!

How vicious the heavens, I dare not extol.

To cloak thyself in love to which does hide a
diabolical nature

How fictitious is thy truth!

Ordaining fiends to wound my youth!

My soul to be confined

as if not by design!

I wage war against thee!

"Enough with your blasphemy!!!" The archangel interrupted.

"Your profanity is the cause of your calamity!

Yet, still by grace the heavens can erase!

I stand here before you, to leave you not alone

Even with all your attempts to dethrone

Love has brought me here, your sin to atone"

"I hate you!!" I screamed and I wept.

The archangel stated his final precept:

"The seed of life is ever buried in the process of suffering.

May thy opposition deteriorate

to thereby enter heaven's gate"

Retribution

The angel did flee to leave me in perpetual misery.

Allowing the demons to take their turn

Scourging my soul, inflicting lashings that burn

Still, I made no concession of guilt

A soul designed only to suffer, I surrender to wilt.

Is that not the true meaning of sacrifice?

To delight in one's own suffering?

For it was God who nailed Jesus to the Cross, not intending to emboss

For God cares not who is deserving or undeserving , saint nor sinner

Hell is the pit for all earth dwellers

I accept my retribution

it is a holy contribution

For what sense is there to fight?

when Heaven has denied respite

Perturbation

Who shall dare justify the ways of God to man?

The ancient trickster

the inferno serpent

Two hearts He had created to be pure and true

To seek the Lord in all thy ways

Adam and Eve vowed to pursue

What had provoked God

To transform into an unholy beast?

To tempt the Divine feminine to deny her virtue
?

To sensationalize her hunger for knowledge,

and to compromise her oath?

For in the darkness God commanded light

And inspired life with all his might

His spirit animated not only Adam and Eve

But birds and the bees

the lowly dragon slithering in the weeds

The Fall of man, God did plan

To disobey God is the fool's folly

But it is also the wise man's calling

Crucifix

The preacher boldly exclaims, “the wage of sin
is death!”

While staring into the eyes of the young girl
with the stained white dress.

With fear she swallowed the apple in her throat.

Then looked up to the man with the bleeding
head and piercing stare

What a heavy price waged against Christ.

God preordained his life a heist

The epitome of holy

The man without sin who fulfilled his duty
wholly

It was God who had instructed Judas to lay the
kiss upon his cheek

Appearing as an act of love, though a mockery
to the meek

Destiny had offered Jesus a sour Chalice

Ever the faithful

He drank without malice

Oh how painfully he wept

every prickly thorn and brass nail felt

That strong wood cross is such a paradox

Symbolizing both heaven and hell,

the marriage of life and death

The union of darkness and light

The Holy Abductor

Possessing no reason or will to fight

I surrendered to this spiritual night.

By Hell's power I have been destroyed

A Divine Operation I could not avoid

So into the abyss, I lay amiss

Until I was awakened by St. John's Kiss

"Your transfigured heart will allow you to feel the warmth of paradise

I will show you how to mortify your senses to forbid all weakness and vice."

I interrupted, "for what reason shall I endure another trial?"

John proceeded, "you have done well to endure this exile

T'is true, God hid himself from you

His chastising hand has been heavy

For the purpose that your soul is cleansed and ready"

John reached out his hand and thereby appeared a large black pegasus

"It is now time to forego satanic interference

Whereas your soul had been cleansed by fire, it will now be cleansed by love"

I had risen and grabbed the hand of the holy knight

I've been granted the opportunity to participate in God's Omnipotence

The fate of my soul now depends on this conductor

Like a thief in the night, he appeared as my holy abductor

We ascended into the 4th dimension of the abyss.

My soul arrived in meek sobriety

Ready to accept my soul's lesson in its entirety

The holy knight led me to a large white veil

"My beloved, it is time to be lead you through this hell"

I crossed the threshold

Ready to endure this spiritual exercise

Soul regeneration my hope to acquiesce

Prudence

The 4th dimension represents spiritual maturity and of stability mind

Designed to lead lost souls to a love that is kind

Providence sent me two soul mates

My heart to decide which one is fate

With whom to spend your life

It is the choice between rapture and strife

I was kissed by a trickster so passionate and sweet

A world wind romance designed to trap me

Foolishly I'd say, "it is he! My twin flame! Although my heart bleeds, he is worth all the pain!"

But then I remembered John's kiss.

The first moment I felt true love's bliss.

For love is free and it is abundant

It will never cost your soul or deem redundant

For prudence is the most cardinal virtue

the wisdom to discern which is false and true

I returned the through the white veil

To meet my holy knight

He stood there proud, strong and might,

John said to me, “You are well on your way to divine ascension.

Take my hand, it is time to enter the third dimension.”

Justice

The 3rd dimension denotes a magical trinity
Of Knowledge, harmony, and supreme divinity
It was there I learned balance
Where Love had granted me a bitter sweet chalice

I crossed the red veil

The virtue of justice to be beheld

This world was full of karma

an endless cycle of lost and gain

there I experienced my fair share of pain

I often dreamed of a double edged sword

Where one end pierced my eye

denoting the power to justly decide

Through my spiritual obedience

I served the highest good of others

And still I was betrayed by my brother

There is much that is hidden within the hearts of man

And still it is wise to trust God's plan

Those who are desperate are the most unjust

Whose words may sound sweet but breeds distrust

Their desperate eye is full of lust

Justice is the delicate balance

of judgment and reason

the ultimate vindicator of treason

Fortitude

I returned through the red veil

To ascend to the 2nd Dimension of hell

John said to me, "you have grown wise in your spiritual character.

All to prepare you to face this mighty barrier.

This dimension will test your faith, but you must not forget the virtue of fortitude."

I spent 30 years in captivity

I was haunted by the most foul and filthy images

And laid witness to the ugliness of death

In this reality, God was foreign to me

I was under the watch of a wicked master

I was left bloody in a field with 72 lashes

In the midst of my suffering, archangel Uriel appeared before me.

“Fix your consciousness on the eternal presence of the Lord.

You must conquer your fear of death

to overcome the world.

Right now you are surrounded by darkness and confusion

But you must know your mortality is only an illusion.

Man can destroy the flesh, but man can not destroy the spirit.

I came to deliver this prophecy, it is good for you to hear it:

In the midst of chaos, God sheds light on truth.

There’s a spiritual purpose for what you are going through.

The time has come for your repent

So you can be redeemed and carried by heaven's best sent

You will spend another 15 years as slave

It will serve you well to be wise and brave

Fear not, my beloved, for heaven will send you aid.

Lean not on your own understanding

For it can result in serious reprimanding

Your affliction is not designed to break you down, yet is designed to break you free"

The angel vanished from me.

Temperance

I died in spiritual glory

And was reborn to tell my story

I returned through the veil.

To ascend to the final dimension of hell.

When I passed through the last veil

I stumbled upon a world full of sensual pleasure and vice

Whereas there were many demons that deceived and enticed

Material gluttony became the director of my descenion

I struggled to maintain spiritual obedience with every decision

But somehow I recalled what John had mentioned:

"Temperance, my love, is the virtue of self control

Clinging to worldly pleasures will surely take its toll

Dare you not forget

To moderate all energy gained and spent

Do not be consumed by your desires

For it is the surest way to return to the pit of fire"

My remembrance of these words allowed me to aim higher.

I did all that was asked of me

To obtain spiritual mastery

I was eager for my communion

To worship in humility, and obtain divine reunion

I underwent a sensual and spiritual purging

the almighty revealed His strength

By overwhelming the darkness with light

And by his grace, I am filled with delight

www.ingramcontent.com/pod-product-compliance
Lightning Source LLC
Chambersburg PA
CBHW051745130826
49812CB00033B/1012
9789357210539